WORKBOOK

FOR

WINTERING

The Power of Rest and Retreat in Difficult Times

(A Practical Guide to Katherine May's Book)

STELLA YAEL

THIS WORKBOOK BELONGS TO

_____

_____

DISCLAIMER

This work is an unofficial workbook of the original book. It is not authorized, sanctioned, licensed or endorsed by the author or publisher of the original book or any of their licenses or affiliates.

HOW TO USE THIS WORKBOOK

Workbook for Wintering has been designed to improve your learning and assist you in understanding the major ideas and concepts covered in the original book more thoroughly. The goal of this section is to help you make the most of your journey toward personal development and introspection by advising you on how to use this workbook effectively.

1. Start with the Summary:
Reading the workbook's Summary section first will help you get a quick overview of the main points and takeaways from the original book. Before reading the remaining chapters, you should have a firm understanding of the book's main message thanks to this summary, which can also act as a reminder or introduction.

2. Explore the Chapters: Each chapter of this workbook focuses on a different subject or concept covered in the original book. Reading the chapter first will help you focus on the important ideas. Spend some time thinking about each lesson and how it relates to your own experiences and beliefs.

3. Practice Self-Reflection: Use the self-reflection prompts provided in each chapter after you've absorbed the key lessons. These inquiries are intended to promote serious contemplation and self-examination, promoting personal development and enabling you to use the information and insights from the original book to improve your own life. Spend some time considering the answers to these questions before filling out the spaces with your reflections. You'll learn more about yourself, your beliefs, and your aspirations as a result of this self-reflection process.

4. Leverage the Self-Evaluation Questions: After you've read through all the chapters and done some introspection, focus on the section of the workbook's end that contains the Self-Evaluation Questions. These questions are intended to assist you in evaluating your development and the ways in which you've applied the book's lessons to your life. To gain insightful knowledge about your own personal development journey, answer these questions honestly and with thought.

5. Review and Revisit: As you work through this workbook, it's crucial to go back and go over your earlier responses and reflections. This will help you keep track of your development, spot trends, and spot

any areas that may need more research or development. You can solidify your personal development by frequently reviewing your previous responses to help you remember the lessons you've learned.

Remember, this workbook is a tool for growth and self- discovery. Accept the process, be receptive to different viewpoints, and give yourself ample time to thoughtfully consider your own experiences. You can get the most out of this workbook and advance your personal development process by paying close attention to the key lessons and self-reflection questions and being open-minded about how you're doing.

The Workbook for Wintering will take you on a transformative journey, and I wish you luck and a rewarding experience.

With Love,
Stell Yael.

SUMMARY

Katherine May's "Wintering: The Power of Rest and Retreat in Difficult Times" focuses on the concept of "wintering" as a metaphor for difficult times in life. The author is inspired by nature, where winter signifies a period of hibernation, relaxation, and renewal. She mixes personal tales, historical references, and cultural insights throughout the book to highlight the importance of embracing and surviving tough seasons.

May begins the story by recounting her own winter experiences, including periods of personal difficulty and the influence they had on her bodily and emotional well-being. The book urges readers to see tough times as essential pauses for reflection and growth rather than failures. May believes that, just as nature needed winter for regeneration, humans may benefit from rest and retreat during difficult times.

One prevalent theme in "Wintering" is the recognition of vulnerability and the significance of reaching out for help. During difficult times, May highlights the importance of community and personal connection. She explains how shared stories and empathy may bring consolation and develop resilience using examples from her own life and the experiences of others.

The book dives into the historical and cultural relevance of wintering, looking at how various communities have addressed and welcomed difficult times. The author explores the rituals and traditions that have developed around the subject of retreat, from ancient practices to current practices. She points out the universality of the wintering experience and the common human urge for repair by fusing different cultural viewpoints.

Furthermore, "Wintering" addresses the cultural pressure to be always productive as well as the shame connected with periods of pause. May questions the prevalent narrative that success is equated with nonstop activity, claiming that relaxation and recharge are essential for long-term well-being. She encourages readers to reconsider their relationship with productivity and to enjoy the ebb and flow of life's seasons via her story.

The book goes deeper into the transforming power of wintering, emphasizing how adversity may lead to personal development and self-discovery. May tells the stories of people who, despite difficulty, discover-red courage and perseverance throughout their wintering adventures. The author advises readers to embrace the transforming potential of challenges by reframing problems as chances for reflection and rebirth.

May uses beautiful language and vivid images to portray the spirit of the seasons throughout "Wintering," emphasizing analogies between the natural world and the human experience. Her writing style is thoughtful and introspective, encouraging readers to think on their own winter travels and find significance in life's cyclical pattern.

In conclusion, Katherine May's "Wintering: The Power of Rest and Retreat in Difficult Times" is a poignant analysis of the human experience of overcoming difficulties. The author urges readers to accept winter as a natural and essential part of life with a combination of personal experience, cultural ideas, and beautiful writing. The book offers a compassionate guide for dealing with challenges, emphasizing on the importance of rest, connection, and self-discovery on the path to regeneration and resilience.

PROLOGUE
September
Indian Summer

This chapter sets the tone for a thoughtful investigation of the transformative power of rest during difficult times. The author draws similarities between the natural world's wintering, a season of dormancy and rebirth, and the human experience of dealing with difficulties. The prologue presents the concept of an Indian Summer, a deceptive time of warmth before the severity of winter that serves as a metaphor for life's unexpected challenges.

May navigates the emotional landscapes of loss, transition, and uncertainty with grace, highlighting the significance of embracing times of rest and retreat. The prologue hints to the overarching theme of finding strength and growth in times of silence, much as nature does throughout the winter.

May inspires readers to reevaluate their relationship with difficulties through her own personal experiences, encouraging a deeper understanding of the healing nature of retreat and the resilience that may emerge from such moments of hibernation.

Key Lessons

1. Embrace the Unexpected: The prologue highlights the significance of an Indian Summer—a deceptive warmth before winter—as a metaphor for life's unforeseen challenges. Instead of resisting unexpected challenges, it encourages readers to embrace and adjust to them.

2. Nature's Wisdom: The author imparts the wisdom of nature's wintering by drawing analogies between human experiences and the natural world. It implies that, like the dormant season, retreat and rest are essential for one's growth and renewal.

3. Reflective Pause: The prologue emphasizes the powerof reflection in tough situations. It helps individuals to take a step back, reflect on their experiences, and find meaning in the pauses, allowing them to have a better understanding of their individual challenges.

4. Resilience through Rest: The author introduces the idea that periods of calm and retreat are typically when strength and resilience arise. In contrast to society's stress on perpetual activity, the prologue implies that genuine power might be discovered in the ability to relax and recuperate.

5. Establishing a Connection with Difficulty: Rather than avoiding or dreading tough times, the prologue proposes making connection with them. Individuals may manage their wintering moments with a sense of purpose and understanding if they acknowledge and face problems.

EXERCISES

1. Unexpected Challenge Reflection Exercise: Identify a recent unexpected challenge or difficulty in your life. Reflect on how you first reacted to it and how embracing the unexpected could have changed your perspective. Make a list of three positive outcomes that emerged from facing this challenge.

_____

_____

_____

_____

_____

_____

2. Nature Connection Exercise: Spend at least 20 minutes in nature, whether it's a park, garden, or natural scenery. Observe the changes in the surroundings, taking note of signs of dormancy or renewal. Examine how these natural cycles connect to the concept of wintering in human life. Think about the lessons nature can teach you about rest and relaxation.

_____

_____

_____

_____

_____

_____

3. Resilience Journaling Exercise: Keep a resilience journal for a week. Each day, write down times when you displayed perseverance or strength during challenging times. Include times of rest or retreat and how they contributed to your capacity to overcome problems. Reflect on the patterns that emerge and how embracing rest may be a source of resilience in your life.

SELF REFLECTION QUESTIONS

How do you typically respond to unexpected challenges in your life, and have there been situations where embracing the unexpected might have resulted in a more positive outcome?

_____

_____

_____

_____

_____

_____

In what ways can you draw inspiration from the natural world's wintering to approach tough times as opportunities for your own growth and renewal?

_____

_____

_____

_____

_____

_____

_____

Reflect on a recent challenging experience and how taking a reflective pause could have influenced your understanding of what was happening. What insights did you gain from this reflection?

_____

_____

_____

_____

_____

_____

_____

How do you perceive the concept of resilience, and in what areas of your life have you discovered strength and growth emerging from moments of stillness and retreat?

_____

_____

_____

_____

_____

_____

In what ways can you engage with difficulties instead of avoiding or being afraid of them? How might this shift in perspective impact your ability to navigate through difficult times?

_____

NOTES

OCTOBER
MAKING READY

In this part, the author dives into the transforming nature of preparation during difficult times in our lives. She highlights the importance of getting ready for the metaphorical winter seasons—those times of reflection, healing, and self-discovery.

The author expertly navigates her own experiences, combining personal storytelling with insightful reflections. She emphasizes the importance of acknowledging and embracing the likelihood of tough times, pushing readers to take a proactive approach in preparing for these inescapable winters. The chapter is a guide on how to emotionally and psychologically prepare for life's challenges.

The author uses the metaphor of winter, a season generally linked with lethargy and hibernation. She encourages individuals to understand the importance of slowing down, taking stock of one's inner resources, and cultivating a resilient attitude. Making ready, according to the author's narrative, entails growing a sense of self-awareness, creating emotional resilience, and accepting the idea that rest and retreat are not signs of weakness but vital instruments for progress.

The chapter resonates with individuals because it examines the universal experience of facing challenges and the significance of preparing for the emotional and psychological aspects that make up these trials.

As individuals journey through "Making Ready," they are guided through an in-depth look on the strategies as well as mindsets that might prepare them for life's inevitable difficulties. The chapter demonstrates the author's conviction in the transforming value of rest and retreat, opposing cultural conventions that generally promote perpetual work.

In a nutshell, "Making Ready" is a road plan for accepting life's cycles, recognizing the importance of wintering, and preparing oneself to emerge stronger from the inevitable hardships that lie ahead.

Key Lessons

1. Embrace life's natural cycles: The chapter "Making Ready" emphasizes the significance of knowing and embracing life's seasonal nature. Just as winter is a time of rest and preparation for spring's development, we must acknowledge that there are times when we must slow down, ponder, and recharge in order to thrive in the future.

2. Recognize the importance of retreating: The chapter highlights the need of retreating and taking time for oneself during tough times. It reminds us that taking a step back from our responsibilities and concentrating on self-care is not a sign of weakness, but rather a crucial step toward healing and progress.

3. Find strength in isolation: The author delves into the transformational power of solitude as well as the opportunity it provides to reconnect with oneself. We have the chance to improve our understanding of who we are, what we actually desire, and how we may go ahead with purpose by being alone.

4. Let go of the urge for control: "Making Ready" teaches us to let go of the need to control every aspect of our life and to instead trust in the natural flow of things. It reminds us that, although there may be uncertainty and difficulties, there will also be beauty and progress in embracing the unknown.

5. Cultivate resilience through rest: The chapter emphasizes the importance of rest and how it adds to our overall resilience. We become better prepared to meet and overcome challenges when we allow ourselves to rest and replenish. It urges us to prioritize self-care and rest as important components of our overall well-being.

EXERCISES

1. Reflection Exercise: Spend some time to reflect on your past "wintering" experiences - times when you encountered tough or trying moments in your life.

Write down what you learnt and how your experiences shaped you as a person.

_____

_____

_____

_____

_____

What methods did you use to get through those trying times?

_____

_____

_____

_____

Is there anything you can take away from past experiences and apply to your present situation?

_____

_____

_____

_____

_____

_____

2. Create a self-care strategy for the next week or month. Think about what activities or practices you find restorative and healing. This might include things like as going for a stroll in nature, practicing meditation or mindfulness, reading a good book, or spending time with family and friends.

Make a list of self-care activities that you can commit to and prioritize in the coming weeks.

_____

_____

_____

_____

_____

_____

3. Gratitude Practice: Make a list of three things you are thankful for. These might be simple joyous moments or experiences, or bigger things in your life that you value.

_____

_____

_____

Reflect on why these things or events are important to you and how they contribute to your overall well-being. Even in challenging situations, this activity can help you develop a sense of gratitude and positive mindset.

SELF REFLECTION QUESTIONS

How have you embraced or resisted the idea of wintering in your own life?

_____

_____

_____

_____

_____

What are some of the most important lessons you've learned from embracing rest and retreat during trying times?

_____

_____

_____

_____

_____

In what ways have you allowed external forces or situations to determine your well-being rather than taking charge of your own self-care and rest?

_____

_____

_____

_____

_____

What are some practical steps you can take to create more intentional spaces for rest and retreat, either in your physical surroundings or inside your own mind and soul?

_____

_____

_____

_____

_____

NOTES

HOT WATER

The author analyzes the transforming impact of hot water and its relevance during tough times in our life in this chapter. She starts by relating a personal event in which her boiler failed during the winter, leaving her without heat or hot water. The event serves as a metaphor for the emotional "wintering" we experience during difficult times.

May explores the history of hot water in many cultures, emphasizing its therapeutic effects and symbolism. Hot water has long been used as a place of rejuvenation and reflection, from Roman bathhouses to Japanese onsen. It functions as a physical and spiritual cleaner, allowing us to relieve tension and find peace in the midst of chaos. Hot water also symbolizes rebirth since it enables us to shed our old selves and emerge renewed.

May then goes into her own hot water experiences, from childhood recollections of her parents' claw-foot tub to the peace she gets in her own hot baths as an adult. According to her, hot water is not just a source of comfort but also a source of inspiration. It frees her mind from the constraints of the outer world. This approach is similar to the concept of "wintering," in which taking time to withdraw and relax provides for reflection and personal improvement.

She also addresses hydrotherapy, a procedure that employs hot water to treat physical illnesses and promote mental health. Water's warmth soothes the body and calms the mind, making it an excellent tool for self-care and healing. This emphasizes the importance of self-care during stressful times, since caring for our physical and mental health is critical for resilience and recovery.

May concludes the chapter by reflecting on the lessons she has learnt from hot water. She realizes that finding small moments of solace and calm in the midst of challenging situations is critical. These moments of rest, whether it's a hot cup of tea or a lengthy soak in the tub, give the fortitude and clarity required to endure challenging circumstances.

Key Lessons

1. The importance of solitude: May emphasizes the importance of finding moments of solitude and embracing them as opportunities for self-reflection and rejuvenation. She discovers the healing power of being alone and the importance of taking the time to listen to her thoughts and emotions.

2. Finding beauty in simplicity: May takes peace in the simple process of boiling water and making a cup of tea. This serves as a reminder that even in terrible situations, we can discover pleasure and beauty in the most little things. We may create a stronger feeling of satisfaction and gratitude by concentrating on the present moment and finding joy in simple routines.

3. The transformational power of rituals: May recognizes how rituals, such as boiling water for a cup of tea, may have a shifting effect on our mental state. Engaging in familiar and comfortable rituals may create a feeling of security and help us find peace in stressful circumstances. By creating routines that bring us delight, we may actively participate in self-care and foster a feeling of well-being.

4. The power of embracing vulnerability: May faces her own vulnerability through her interactions with hot water and the emotions it evokes in her. She realizes that vulnerability is not something to be dreaded, but rather a natural part of the human experience. Accepting and embracing vulnerability allows us to be open to growth and connection with others. We can only discover strength and resilience through vulnerability.

5. Finding strength in nature: May considers the healing power of nature, symbolized by the steam rising from the kettle. She takes peace in the changing seasons, the beauty of fall, and the cycles of life that nature depicts. Connecting with nature may provide us with perspective, grounding, and a reminder of the greater world outside our personal difficulties. We might find solace and fresh optimism by immersing ourselves in nature.

SELF REFLECTION QUESTIONS

How has finding warmth in daily activities helped you in navigating difficult times in your life?

_____

_____

_____

_____

_____

Did the idea of embracing pain and finding beauty in the ordinary strike a chord with you? If yes, how have you applied it in your daily life?

_____

_____

_____

_____

_____

Reflect on a time when you refused to rest or retreat and how it affected your general well-being. In the future, how will you create time for rest?

_____

_____

_____

_____

_____

_____

_____

How can embracing seasonal changes, both
outwardly and inwardly, lead to personal growth
and resilience?

_____

_____

_____

_____

_____

_____

_____

Have you ever experienced moments of unexpected joy or inspiration while doing boring tasks? How can you bring more of these experiences into your life?

_____

_____

_____

_____

_____

Consider how you might actively seek warmth and comfort, even in the midst of challenging situations. What practical efforts can you take to instill a sense of comfort and ease?

_____

_____

_____

_____

NOTES

GHOST STORIES

The author explores the theme of facing one's fears and the power of storytelling in the midst of difficulties in this chapter.

She clearly describes October as a month when darkness descends and the world around us seems to change. She makes use of Halloween symbolism, a time when we address and face our fears through ghost stories and costumes.

To illustrate her point, the author recalls a childhood incident in which her younger sister, Sophie, had a frightening experience with a ghost. Sophie was terrified, unable to express her fear, and haunted by the the incident. The author delves into this memory in order to understand Sophie's silence and assist her in confronting her ghosts.

She addresses the significance of sharing stories throughout the chapter, highlighting how it may give the tools needed for healing and growth. She proposes that we all carry our own ghosts, fears, and pain, and that we may find peace and strength by weaving these stories into stories of resilience and transformation.

May also reflects on her personal experiences with fear and how writing and sharing her stories has helped her cope. She points out the importance of identifying and embracing our fears rather than suppressing or ignoring them. She claims that this method helps us to confront our ghosts and discover solutions to heal and move ahead.

In addition, she explores liminal spaces, which are times in our lives when we feel lonely, disoriented, and unsure. Drawing on her own "wintering" experiences, May highlights the importance of embracing these moments of seclusion and relaxation, as they often lead to self-discovery and personal development.

Finally, the author brilliantly weaves together personal anecdotes, psychological insights, and the power of storytelling to examine the issue of addressing fears and finding resilience in difficult times. She encourages individuals to accept their own ghosts, tell their stories, and find strength in the face of tragedy.

Key Lessons

1. Embrace the power of storytelling: The chapter emphasizes the importance of ghost stories in our lives. It teaches us that through storytelling, we can explore our fears, worries, and hidden emotions in a safe and controlled environment. We may better understand ourselves and find peace even in the darkest of situations by interacting with these stories.

2. Acknowledge and accept the presence of darkness and uncertainty in our lives: The chapter's lesson is to identify and accept the existence of darkness and uncertainty in our lives. Just as winter is an unavoidable part of the natural cycle, so are tough times and obstacles. We may build resilience and discover power within ourselves by accepting and embracing our dark side.

3. Find comfort in the eerie and unknown: This chapter delves into the soothing power of eerie atmospheres and mystery stories. It implies that experiencing these uncomfortable elements might provide a feeling of comfort and catharsis. Instead of avoiding difficulty, we might lean into it to find peace and inspiration.

4. Seek rest and retreat: The chapter points out the importance of rest and retreat during trying times. Just as fall invites nature into a period of hibernation and introspection, we, too, need stillness and withdrawal to recover and process our experiences. Resting helps us to recover, reflect, and eventually emerge stronger.

5. Connect with nature's cycles: The chapter encourages us to connect with and align ourselves with nature's cycles. We may learn significant lessons about impermanence, resilience, and the cyclical nature of life by watching the changing seasons. This understanding allows us to enjoy the ebb and flow of our own experiences, as well as find meaning and direction in the natural world around us.

SELF REFLECTION QUESTIONS

How has your fear of uncertainty and change affected your ability to adapt and welcome new experiences?

_____

_____

_____

_____

_____

_____

In light of the concept of finding refuge in our own minds, how have you actively sought to create a mental sanctuary during difficult times?

_____

_____

_____

_____

_____

_____

Have you truly allowed yourself to embrace the transformative power of grief and loss in shaping your personal growth and how you view the world around you?

_____

_____

_____

_____

In what ways have you intentionally sought silence and stillness to reconnect with your inner self and find clarity in the midst of the noise and bustle of everyday life?

_____

_____

_____

_____

NOTES

NOVEMBER

METAMORPHOSIS

The chapter explores the idea of progress and transformation amid challenging situations. The author opens the chapter by describing the change of seasons from autumn to winter, highlighting the bleakness and coldness of November. She describes how this transition mirrors her own personal losses and struggles.

The author delves into the idea of "wintering", a term she uses to describe "periods of retreat and rest required for personal growth and renewal." She reflects on her own winter experiences, especially during the month of November, and how they have served as a catalyst for change in her life. She compares this process to the metamorphosis of a caterpillar into a butterfly, highlighting the discomfort and vulnerability that may accompany change.

The theme of solitude and the significance of allowing oneself to be alone is also explored by the author. She understands that, although solitude may be unpleasant and even painful at times, it can also provide a place for self-reflection and personal growth. May shares her personal experiences with solitude over the month of November, and how it enabled her to confront her fears and gain clarity.

May weaves her own story with vulnerability and resilience throughout the chapter. She discusses how she has learnt to embrace difficulties and turn it into an opportunity for growth and transformation.

During challenging circumstances, the author also emphasizes the importance of rest and self-care. She understands that it might be tempting to go on, but underlines the need to listen to one's body and taking a step back when necessary. She talks about her personal experiences with rest and introspection over the month of November, and how they helped her refresh and gain perspective.

In conclusion, the chapter delves into the idea of transformation and progress during challenging periods. The author reflects on her own winter experiences and the lessons she learnt from solitude and self-care. She encourages individuals to accept the discomfort that comes with change and to use these moments for personal regeneration. Finally, November becomes a symbolic month of metamorphosis and resilience.

Key Lessons

1. Accepting and embracing change: The chapter emphasizes the importance of accepting and embracing change in our life. We may find strength in allowing ourselves to transform and grow during difficult times, just like nature does throughout the winter.

2. The beauty of stillness and retreat: The month of November is associated with hibernation and stillness. The chapter highlights the need of taking time for retreat and rest, enabling us to find peace and refreshment in quiet times.

3. Accepting and finding beauty in darkness: November is known for its long nights and darkness. Instead of resisting or fearing the darkness, the lesson urges us to discover beauty and significance in it. By embracing the darkness, we may be able to uncover hidden depths within ourselves as well as gain insights that we would not have discovered in the light.

4. Resilience in the face of challenges: The chapter highlights the significance of persistence in tough times, just as nature survives the challenges of winter. It tells us that even when the season seems harsh, th-

ere is always the possibility of growth and rejuvenation if we can have the will to continue.

5. The power of community and interconnectedness: Many natural creatures migrate and gather in communal spaces in November. This chapter teaches the importance of community and connectivity. It reminds us of the power and support we may find by coming together, sharing our troubles, and finding consolation in the company of others during difficult times.

EXERCISES

Exercise 1: Personal transformation reflection.
Instructions:
 - Think about a significant period of transformation or change in your life. It might be a difficult time or a positive shift that brought about growth and advancemen
Reflect on the emotions, struggles, and successes you encountered throughout this time
Journal about your transformation, concentrating on the following points:

How has this transformation impacted your life and perspective?

_____

_____

_____

_____

What lessons did you take away from this experience?

_____

_____

_____

_____

How did this moment of transformation shape the person you are today?

_____

_____

_____

_____

Take a time to appreciate the strength and resilience that emerged from your metamorphosis.
Carry this reflection with you throughout the day to remind yourself of the power of transformation.

Exercise 2: Embracing Uncertainty and Accepting Change.
Instructions:

- Bring to mind a recent situation or period in your life in which you faced uncertainty or resistance to change.
- It might be a personal relationship, a work-related issue, or any other part of your life.
-Reflect on your initial reaction to the uncertainty or change.

Did you resist it or try to control the outcome? How did it make you feel?

_____

_____

_____

_____

_____

Change your perspective by asking yourself, "What opportunities or possibilities might emerge from this uncertainty or change?"

_____

_____

_____

_____

How can you welcome the uncertainty and view it as an opportunity for growth and transformation?

_____

_____

_____

_____

- Take a minute to jot down any new thoughts or views you've gained from this exercise.
- Practice letting go of the demand for certainty and control by participating in activities that promote flexibility and adaptability.

-This might include attempting new activities, exploring different perspectives, or taking little steps outside of your comfort zone.

-Repeat this exercise anytime you experience doubt or resistance to change, using it as a chance to broaden your mentality and embrace the transforming potential of uncertainty.

SELF REFLECTION QUESTIONS

Have you ever felt resistance or fear towards change, and if so, how did you work through those emotions to embrace the potential for growth and transformation?

_____

_____

_____

_____

_____

What role does rest and retreat play in your own life, and how might consciously embracing these practices enhance your ability to engage with and surrender to the process of transformation?

_____

_____

_____

_____

_____

How can you cultivate a sense of curiosity and openness towards the unknown, rather than clinging to certainty and familiarity, when facing periods of change and transition?

_____

_____

_____

_____

_____

_____

What steps can you take to create intentional spaces and rituals for rest and retreat in your own life, in order to nourish and support your journey of personal transformation?

_____

_____

_____

_____

_____

NOTES

SLUMBER

The author delves into the concept of slumber as an essential aspect of the human experience. She explores the idea of slumber not just as a physical act of sleeping, but also as a metaphorical state of withdrawing and hibernating during difficult times.

May starts by recounting her personal experience with a chronic illnesses that left her exhausted and in constant need of rest. She reflects on how society often views rest as a luxury or a sign of laziness, but she argues that it is during these periods of slumber that profound healing and growth occur. Slumber is a transformative time for May because it forces us to slow down and pay attention to our needs, allowing us to recharge both physically and emotionally.

The author examines the numerous ways in which slumber can manifest in our lives. It can take the form of a physical illness or injury that forces us to take a break from our daily routines. A loss or a time of sadness might leave us feeling exhausted and in need of solitude. She suggests that these moments of slumber be viewed as opportunities for introspection and self-discovery rather than as setbacks.

The author also looks into the historical and cultural significance of slumber, using examples from mythology and literary works. She references the Greek myth of Persephone, who spends half the year in the underworld during the winter, symbolizing the necessary period of rest and renewal. May claims that our society has lost touch with the value of slumber because we are constantly pressured to be productive and always on the go.

May emphasizes the significance of embracing slumber as a necessary part of the human experience, emphasizing the benefits that can result from these periods of rest. She claims that slumber helps us to confront our fears and weaknesses, ultimately leading to personal growth and transformation. May emphasizes that slumber should not be viewed as a sign of weakness, but rather as a natural and necessary response to the difficult situations.

In conclusion, this chapter delves into the concept of slumber as a transformative time of rest and retreat. The author encourages individuals to view these periods of slumber, whether forced or voluntary, as opportunities for personal growth and reflection. By reevaluating our societal norms and understanding the importance of rest, she argues that we can navigate difficult times with more resilience and embrace the healing power of slumber.

Key Lessons

1. The importance of rest: The chapter highlights the value of rest and sleep in our lives, especially during stressful times. It emphasizes the concept of rest as a requirement for our well-being rather than a luxury. We can better manage difficult times if we recognize our need for rest and give ourselves permission to slow down.

2. Respecting the body's natural cycles: This chapter delves into the topic of circadian rhythms and how they influence our sleeping patterns. It encourages us to pay heed to our body's signals and work with rather than against our natural cycles. We may improve our overall health and resilience by recognizing our body's demand for rest and sleep.

3. The power of dreams and subconscious processing: "Slumber" examines the role of dreams and the subconscious mind in our mental and emotional processing. It emphasizes the necessity of giving our dreams room and attention, as they may contain significant insights and provide advice during tough times. We may access our inner knowledge and disco-

ver insight in difficult times by paying attention to our dreams.

4. Letting go of perfectionism: The chapter covers the difficulties that come with aiming for perfection in our sleep and rest practices. It points out the dangers of putting yourself under pressure and having unrealistic expectations. Instead of striving for perfect sleep or uninterrupted rest, the author advocates embracing the flaws and realizing that slumber, like life, may be chaotic and unexpected. We may create a more compassionate and nurturing relationship with ourselves and our relaxation routines by letting go of perfectionism.

5. Finding peace in solitude: "Slumber" delves into the importance of solitude and calm reflection during moments of rest. It highlights the significance of devoting time to reflection solitude away from constant stimulation and other distractions. We may connect with our inner selves, find solace, and replenish our energies by creating moments of quietness.

EXERCISE

Exercise 1: Reflect on Your Own Winter Experience
Instructions:
1. Take some quiet time to think about a tough moment in your life when you believed you were in a "wintering" phase.
2. Describe your experience in full, including the emotions you had, the problems you experienced, and any lessons you learnt.
3. Examine your approach to your wintering experience.

Did you resist it, or did you accept it? Did you give yourself time to relax and recharge, or did you press through without allowing yourself to heal?

----

4. Think about what you might have done differently to handle that wintering period more effectively and discover greater strength in rest and retreat.

5. Finally, make a list of three specific activities you may take in the future to honor and support yourself throughout the times of winter.

Exercise 2: Create a plan for a "Winter Retreat."
Instructions:

1. Imagine a future wintering season in your life, whether it's something difficult you're anticipating or just a time when you need to rest and withdraw.

2. Make a list of activities or routines that provide you with comfort, tranquility, and energy. Reading, writing, taking baths, going on walks, meditating, or indulging in artistic hobbies are examples of such activities.

3. Make time in your calendar to prioritize these tasks when you begin your next wintering period. Set aside time each day or designating particular days as "retreat days" to concentrate on self-care and refreshment.

4. Identify any possible roadblocks or diversions that may hinder you from completely enjoying your winter retreat plan. Develop coping strategies, such as establishing limits, obtaining help from loved ones, or creating a tranquil atmosphere at home.

5. Make a plan for your winter retreat plan and put it

it somewhere visible. Make a deliberate effort to lean into this strategy and honor your need for rest and retreat when the time comes.

Exercise 3: Develop a Mindful Sleep Routine
Instructions:
1. Begin by evaluating your existing sleeping habits. Consider the behaviors and practices that may be influencing your sleep quality.

Do you always go to bed and wake up at the same time? Are you resting before going to bed, or are you stimulating your mind with devices and professional tasks?

_____

_____

_____

_____

2. Examine several ways for developing a mindful sleep pattern that promotes peaceful sleep. Establishing a nighttime routine, creating a peaceful atmosphere in your bedroom, limiting screen time before bed, and practicing relaxation methods such as deep breathing or gentle stretching may all contribute

to this.

3. Try integrating these ideas into your bedtime routine for at least two weeks. Keep track of any changes in your sleep quality, mood when you wake up, and general energy levels throughout the day.

4. Think about the influence of these changes on your well-being and make any necessary adjustments to your routine. Certain habits or tactics may work better for you than others.

5. Make a long-term strategy for maintaining a mindful sleeping pattern. Setting regular sleep and waking hours, including relaxation activities into your nighttime routine, and establishing a sleep-friendly atmosphere in your bedroom are all examples of this. Revisit and review your routine on a regular basis to ensure that it continues to assist your sleep and general well-being.

SELF REFLECTION QUESTIONS

How have you previously opposed the acceptance of "slumber" in your own life?

_____

_____

_____

_____

_____

_____

Have you ever felt secluded or disconnected
from the world during a "slumber" moment in
your life? If so, how did you handle the
situation and what did you learn from it?

_____

_____

_____

_____

_____

_____

The author emphasizes the importance of seeing sleep as a chance for personal growth and transformation. How can you use this approach in your own life to better embrace restful periods?

_____

_____

_____

_____

_____

_____

_____

_____

_____

NOTES

DECEMBER
LIGHT

The author addresses the transforming power of the winter season and the importance of embracing darkness in order to find inner light in this chapter.

The author starts by reflecting on her childhood memories of Christmas, a season of celebration and pleasure, but also of shortest days and longest nights. She compares the external darkness of winter to the mental darkness that we all experience at difficult times. She suggests that by embracing this darkness, we will be able to find the metaphorical light that will guide us through our struggles.

The author then dives into the Japanese aesthetic concept of wabi-sabi, which welcomes imperfection and transience. She explains that wabi-sabi teaches us to recognize the beauty in decay and to respect our own imperfections and scars. Even in the face of hardship, we may discover a sense of gratitude by accepting our imperfections.

May introduces the idea of hygge, a Danish term for warmth, comfort, and satisfaction. She emphasizes the importance of providing a warm and pleasant environment to retire to throughout the cold months. It might be as easy as lighting candles, cuddling up in blankets, and drinking hot beverages. We may create a feeling of sanctuary that helps us to relax and rejuvenate by making our surroundings comfortable and loving.

The chapter then delves into the importance of light in the dark. The author covers light festivals such as Diwali and Hanukkah, where sending light into the darkness is a sign of hope and rejuvenation. She emphasizes that even in the darkest of circumstances, there are rays of hope that may lead us forward.

May also highlights the importance of discovering light inside ourselves. She proposes that by concentrating on the tiny moments of pleasure and beauty in our life, we may create an inner light that will sustain us throughout tough times. This might be as easy as appreciating the flavor of a tasty meal or the sound of laughing.

The author finishes the chapter by focusing on the concept that winter is a season of metamorphosis, when nature retreats and regenerates in preparation for spring. She recommends that we, too, might enjoy this time of rest and retreat, slowing down, reflecting, and healing.

In conclusion, the chapter encourages individuals to see winter as a time of change and rest, a time to refresh and regain inner strength.

Key Lessons

1. Embrace the darkness: The author highlights the significance of embracing the darkness. The winter months are typically associated with emotions of solitude and silence. Rather of resisting or avoiding these emotions, the author advocates leaning into them and seeking peace in the quiet times. We may learn to appreciate and find beauty in the stillness of winter by embracing the darkness.

2. Find joy in simplicity: December is a month full with festive celebrations and materialistic excess. The author, on the other hand, urges individuals to find pleasure and fulfillment in simplicity. She advocates concentrating on the modest joys and pleasures that may be found in daily moments rather than aiming for big celebrations. A cup of hot chocolate or a quiet walk in the snow might provide more joy than lavish parties or material possessions.

3. Nurture meaningful relationships: The chapter highlights the importance of nurturing meaningful ties in the chapter, especially during the holiday sea-

son. It emphasizes the value of spending time with loved ones, whether they be family, friends, or neighbors. We may experience a sense of belonging and support during difficult times by fostering these connections and engaging in honest conversations.

4. Practice self-compassion: During challenging times, the chapter highlights the importance of practicing self-compassion. The author advises that instead of continually pushing ourselves to achieve and be productive, we should allow ourselves to rest and retreat. We may replenish our energy and find inner strength to navigate challenges by being kind and compassionate to ourselves.

5. Appreciate nature's beauty: Finally, the chapter highlights the beauty and significance of nature throughout the winter months. It encourages individuals to spend time in nature, especially in the winter months. Connecting with nature can bring a sense of awe and perspective, whether it's admiring the winter landscapes or observing the resilience of plants and animals. Appreciating the beauty of the natural world may also serve as a reminder that even in difficult times, there is always room for rebirth and progress.

SELF REFLECTION QUESTIONS

How can you create moments of light and brightness in the midst of the darkness and wintering?

_____

_____

_____

_____

_____

Have you been resisting or embracing the concept of rest and hibernation during difficult times? What effect has this had on your ability to heal and recover?

_____

_____

_____

_____

_____

How can you include nature's healing power and natural light into your everyday routine, particularly during the winter months?

_____

_____

_____

_____

_____

In light of the concept of "luxury of darkness," what mindful activities can you do to fully appreciate and make the most of dark times in your life?

_____

_____

_____

_____

_____

In what way have you found beauty and solace in the contrast between light and darkness, and how can you use this perspective to handle future challenges?

_____

_____

_____

_____

How can you actively create spaces of warmth, light, and comfort in your physical environment to support your emotional well-being during difficult times?

_____

_____

_____

_____

NOTES

MIDWINTER

The author begins with discussing the arrival of winter in both nature and our personal life. She describes how wintering is an important aspect of the natural cycle, when nature rests and regenerates in preparation for the approaching spring. Similarly, she contends that people need moments of rest and seclusion in order to recover and flourish.

May goes into the concept of wintering by recounting her own personal experiences with adversity and the invaluable lessons she learnt from them. She focuses on her problems with chronic sickness as well as the cultural pressure to be active and occupied at all times. She points out that it is at these difficult times that we may reconnect with ourselves, review our goals, and let go of the incessant desire to hustle.

The author also highlights the need of isolation in the winter. She explains how being alone may be seen as a gift rather than a burden since it allows for reflection and self-discovery. May discusses her own experiences of seeking solitude in nature and the therapeutic benefits of spending time alone in winter settings. She proposes that the natural environment may act as a teacher, demonstrating the beauty of stillness and teaching us to observe and pay attention rather than being constantly in motion.

The author then delves into the concept of community and how it may play an important part in wintering. She recognizes that, although solitude is vital, having a support system of kindred spirits who can bring comfort and understanding during tough times is also crucial. She highlights the importance of reaching out to others, sharing our experiences, and lending a helping hand to those who are going through their own winters.

The author discusses the concept of acceptance as a vital part of wintering at the conclusion of the chapter. She contends that rather of battling the terrible times, we should learn to accept them and discover beauty in the darkness. May thinks that, just as winter ultimately gives way to spring, our personal winters will pass and usher forth fresh development and opportunities.

Finally, May's winter adventure serves as a reminder that rest and retreat are not indicators of weakness, but rather necessary components of our total well-being and resilience.

Key Lessons

1. Accept and embrace the darkness: "Midwinter" emphasizes the significance of accepting and embracing the darkness in our lives. Just as the natural world survives the longest and coldest nights during midwinter, we must acknowledge and embrace the challenging and hard times in our own life. These are the periods when we may actually learn and grow.

2. Find beauty in small moments: "Midwinter" emphasizes the importance of finding beauty in small moments, despite the bleakness of winter. Whether it's observing the complex patterns of frost on a window or relaxing with a cup of hot chocolate, these tiny pleasures may provide comfort and enjoyment even in the darkest of times.

3. Give yourself permission to rest and retreat: Winter is a season of rest and retreat in nature, and the same idea applies to our personal life. "Midwinter" highlights the need of giving oneself time to relax and refresh. We may discover the power and resilience to tackle obstacles and go ahead by allowing ourselves to slow down and recuperate.

4. Find solace in nature: This chapter examines the

relationship between people and the natural world throughout the winter months. It reminds us of nature's soothing and restorative benefits on our mental health. Spending time in nature may bring serenity, tranquility, and a feeling of grounding during stressful times, whether it be a stroll in the cool winter air or just witnessing the beauty of a snow-covered landscape.

5. Accept the cyclical nature of life: "Midwinter" reminds us that winter is not a permanent condition, but rather a part of life's cyclical rhythm. Just like the natural world goes through the seasons, our lives go through ups and downs. We may find hope and resilience by understanding that terrible times are merely a part of the larger cycle, and that better days will return.

SELF REFLECTION QUESTIONS

How have you historically dealt with challenges in the past? Are you more likely to push through and dismiss your own need for rest and retreat, or are you more receptive to slowing down and completely experiencing these times?

_____

_____

_____

_____

_____

How do you fight or struggle with the concept of rest and retreat? Is your resistance influenced by underlying beliefs or cultural pressures?

_____

_____

_____

_____

_____

Think about the advantages of rest and retreat in terms of solitude and connecting with oneself. Have you ever intentionally sought isolation during a difficult time? If not, why not? If yes, what did you learn about yourself or your situation?

_____

_____

_____

_____

_____

_____

Are there specific rituals or traditions outlined in the chapter "Midwinter" that you would want to explore or adopt into your own life? How might these practices help you throughout your own winter experiences?

_____

_____

NOTES

EPIPHANY

The author dives further into the theme of epiphany and how it pertains to the wintering process in this chapter.

She explores the transformational nature of epiphanies and how they might emerge during times of solitude and peace.

An epiphany, according to May, is a sudden insight or knowledge, akin to a bolt of lightning illuminating our path. She explains that these epiphanies often occur during periods of pause or withdrawal, when we give ourselves the space and time to reflect. These epiphanies serve as transformation and growth catalysts, moving us ahead on our journey.

Wintering, according to the author, might enhance the occurrence of epiphanies since it encourages introspection. Individuals are more aware of their own thoughts and emotions during this phase of wintering, when they dig down and concentrate on self-care. She describes her own winter experiences and how they enabled her to face her fears and doubts, leading to significant epiphanies about her own identity and purpose.

The author also points out the importance of embracing isolation throughout the wintering period. She claims that being alone allows us to fully listen to ourselves and access our inner wisdom. Epiphanies often occur in these calm times of isolation. May tells examples of how she intentionally sought out periods of solitude, whether through walking in nature or retreating to a cabin, and how these moments lead to significant life breakthroughs.

Furthermore, the author explores the idea that epiphanies are neither linear or predictable. They may be frustrating and elusive, appearing when least anticipated. May recalls how her personal epiphanies often came in situations of vulnerability and discomfort, when she was forced to confront her fears and doubts head on.

Finally, this chapter dives into the significance of epiphanies throughout the winter season. May stresses the transformative nature of these moments of clarity, as well as the significance of solitude and self-reflection in facilitating their occurrence. The author encourages individuals to enjoy the process of wintering and be open to the unexpected insights that might emerge during these seasons of rest and retreat through personal experiences and reflections.

Key Lessons

1. The importance of Slowing Down: The chapter "Epiphany" highlights the importance of slowing down and listening to our own hearts and instincts. In a world that often glorifies busyness and productivity, taking the time for rest and retreat may lead to profound self-discovery and personal growth.

2. Embracing Change: The chapter explores the concept that difficult situations might serve as catalysts for change. We may discover strength and resilience in the face of hardship by embracing the inevitability of change and acknowledging the lessons it offers.

3. The Healing Power of Nature: The chapter emphasizes nature's healing powers and the restorative effects it has on our well-being. Being in nature helps us to connect with something larger than ourselves, providing solace, perspective, and a sense of belonging.

4. Mindfulness Practice: The chapter encourages individuals to embrace the present moment by practicing mindfulness. We cancan deepen our understanding of ourselves and find peace amidst chaos by paying attention to the sensations, thoughts,

and emotions that arise.

5. Authentic Self-Reflection: "Epiphany" highlights self-reflection as a key tool for personal growth. We may get a better understanding of our values, desires, and fears through honest reflection, leading to a more authentic and fulfilling life. The author reveals that difficult situations may provide opportunity for important self-reflection and reevaluation of our goals.

SELF REFLECTION QUESTIONS

What are some areas of your life where you can invite greater vulnerability and connectedness during times of personal growth or change?

_____

_____

_____

_____

_____

How can you cultivate a sense of gratitude and appreciation for the seasons of life, both the joyful and the challenging?

_____

_____

_____

_____

_____

How does the author's exploraton of the power of slowing down and embracing rest challenge any preconceived thoughts or beliefs you may have about productivity and success?

_____

_____

_____

_____

_____

_____

In what ways have you experienced personal
epiphanies or moments of clarity during times
of rest and retreat?

_____

_____

_____

_____

_____

_____

_____

NOTES

JANUARY
DARKNESS

In this chapter, the author digs into the transformative potential of embracing darkness and the winter season. She opens the chapter by recounting her January experience, which often has a connection with gloom and depression. She emphasizes how society often perceives darkness as undesirable, and how we want to numb and distract ourselves from it. May, on the other hand, believes that darkness may be an opportunity for growth and self-reflection.

May highlights the concept of "wintering," which she defines as moments in our life when we face difficult times or feel trapped and down. She draws analogies between nature and our own inner struggles, pointing out how winter enables nature to rest and rejuvenate, resulting in a more vibrant spring. Using personal experiences, the author discusses how she has welcomed winter by making time for reflection, rest, and nourishment. She encourages individuals to do the same, to find peace in the winter's stillness and darkness.

The author also explores today's cultural obsession

with positivity and perpetual productivity. She highlights the significance of allowing oneself to feel negative emotions and acknowledging that they have value as well as purpose. May provides insights from psychological research that show that embracing and processing unpleasant emotions may lead to better resilience and emotional well-being.

The author delves into the concept of "hygge," a Danish term for a feeling of coziness and comfort that she feels can be discovered in embracing the darkness and silence of winter. She discusses the importance of rituals and simple pleasures in providing warmth and solace throughout the winter months. These rituals can be as simple as lighting candles, drinking hot beverages, or spending time with loved ones.

In summary, the author explores the transforming potential of wintering and embracing darkness. She challenges societal norms and encourages individuals to find comfort, reflection, and inspiration amid the stillness of winter.

Key Lessons

1. Embrace darkness: The chapter points out the importance of acknowledging and accepting the presence of darkness in our life. It signifies that darkness is not necessarily unpleasant or to be feared, but rather a natural part of the human experience. By embracing darkness, we are able to navigate difficult times with more resilience and understanding.

2. The cycle of darkness and light: The chapter delves into the cyclical nature of darkness and light, drawing analogies to the changing seasons. Just as winter is required for spring's regrowth and renewal, periods of darkness and solitude may provide us with valuable opportunities for self-reflection, personal development, and eventual restoration.

3. Permission to rest: In a society that often values constant productivity and busyness, the chapter advises individuals to give themselves permission to rest and take breaks as required. It highlights the need of slowing down, allowing oneself to withdraw, and embracing moments of rest necessary for personal well-being and resilience.

4. The power of solitude: The chapter emphasizes the transformative power of solitude during times of darkness. It highlights the need of carving out intentional moments of isolation, away from the noise and pressures of the outside world. Solitude may give a chance for self-discovery, introspection, and healing, allowing people to reconnect with themselves and gain inner strength.

5. Finding meaning in darkness: The chapter explores the concept that darkness may have significant meaning and valuable lessons. It encourages individuals to seek the wisdom and growth that may come from challenges. Individuals may gain new insights, build resilience, and eventually find meaning and purpose in their life by embracing darkness and actively interacting with the difficulties it provides.

EXERCISE

Finding brightness in the midst of darkness

Objective: To recognize and appreciate the moments of light that shine through even in the darkest of circumstances.

Recall a recent difficult experience or a challenging time in your life. In your mind, picture the experience as a dark space.

Now think about any moments of lights or small victories you encountered during that period. It could be moments of joy, support from loved ones, personal growth or any positive experiences that emerged from the darkness.

As you reflect on these moments, imagine them as points of light bursting through the darkness. Envision these points of light becoming brighter and spreading, gradually lighting the darkness more and more.

Write down these moments of light and how they made you feel.

_____

_____

_____

_____

_____

_____

Reflect on how embracing the darkness leads you to discover and appreciate the bright spots in your life.

SELF REFLECTION QUESTIONS

Can you recall a specific time in your life when you went through a period of darkness or difficulty? How did you get through that period, and did you gain anything from it?

_____

_____

_____

_____

_____

_____

In what ways do you tend to avoid or resist facing the darkness or difficult feelings in your life? Are there any patterns or practices that you can identify that contribute to this avoidance?

_____

_____

_____

_____

_____

Reflect on the concept of "transformation in the dark" as explained in the chapter. Can you think of any times in your life when you experienced personal growth or a change in perspective during a difficult time?

_____

_____

_____

_____

_____

How can you implement the concept of embracing darkness and making room for rest and retreat into your everyday life? Are there any particular habits or practices you may adopt to help you handle challenging situations more effectively?

_____

_____

_____

NOTES

HUNGER

In this chapter, the author examines the concept of hunger and its different forms. She starts by reflecting on how nature's resources become few during the winter months, forcing creatures to hibernate or migrate in order to live. Similarly, humans experience an entirely different kind of hunger during these times- a hunger for warmth, comfort, and connection.

The author addresses how our modern society often neglects the importance of rest and retreat, resulting in a disconnection from the natural rhythms. She emphasizes the importance of listening to our body and giving in to the desire for rest when it comes. We may reach a deeper dimension of being and recharge our energy by allowing ourselves to slow down.

The author goes on to explore the hungerfor creativity and how it might be stifled in a culture that sets an excessive emphasis on productivity. She advises individuals to use the winter months for creative reflection and to realize the importance of solitude and stillness in the creative process.

May also examines the importance of emotional connection and the difficulties that come during the winter months, when individuals often feel alone and

and lonely. During these difficult times, she emphasizes the importance of reaching out to people and creating supporting groups. She recommends that modest acts of kindness and actively searching out opportunities to connect with others might satisfy the hunger for connection.

The chapter additionally looks into the hunger for growth and self-improvement, focusing on the idea that growth does not necessarily have to be linear or continuously reaching for more. The author believes that growth may occur during moments of solitude and retreat when we are forced to face our weaknesses and limits.

Finally, the author examines the hunger for hope and resilience in the face of adversity. She reflects on her own winter experiences and how, despite the difficulties, she discovered moments of beauty and hope. She also encourages individuals to believe that winter is just temporary and that spring will eventually come.

In summary, this chapter explores the different forms of hunger that arise throughout the winter months. The author suggests that by embracing rest, creativity, connection, growth, and hope, we can navigate these difficult periods and discover beauty and resilience even in the depths of winter. The chapter serves as a reminder to honor life's natural rhythms and understand that periods of rest and retreat are important for our well-being and personal growth.

Key Lessons

1. Accept and embrace the seasons of life: The chapter highlights the importance of accepting and embracing the difficult seasons we face in life. Just as nature slows down in the winter, it is important to recognize that these difficult periods may provide significant lessons and opportunities for growth.

2. Lean into discomfort: The chapter addresses the concept of hunger, both the physical sense and the metaphorical craving for something greater. We may examine and understand the root causes of discomfort by allowing ourselves to sit with it, whether it be desire for food, connection, or satisfaction. Rather than avoiding pain, leaning into it may lead to self-discovery and growth.

3. Seek nourishment: The chapter highlights the importance of seeking nourishment in various forms. Beyond food, nourishment, can be found in relationships, nature, creativity, and personal hobbies. The author encourages individuals to find

what actually nourishes their spirit and prioritize these sources of sustenance in their lives.

4. Practice mindfulness and gratitude: The chapter highlights the importance of being present and appreciative for what we have, especially in times of scarcity or challenges. We become more aware of the beauty and simple joys in our surroundings as we cultivate a mindful attitude. This practice can help alleviate feelings of hunger or lack by focusing on the abundance that exists in our life.

5. Embrace solitude and rest: The chapter emphasizes the importance of isolation and rest, especially during difficult times. Just as nature withdraws and hibernates during the winter, we can benefit from moments of rest and retreat as well. Taking time for ourselves helps us to refuel, reflect, and recover our energy, resulting in a higher feeling of well-being and resilience while facing challenging situations.

EXERCISE AND SELF-REFLECTION QUESTIONS

Exercise: Reflect on Personal Hunger

Objective: To explore our personal hunger and its underlying causes.

Instruction:
Recall a period when you were hungry not just physically but also emotionally, mentally, or spiritually. It might be a recent experience or something from your past.
Write down your reflections on the following questions:

What were the circumstances or triggers that led to this hunger? Was it a specific event, relationship, or situation?

_____

_____

_____

_____

_____

_____

How did this hunger manifest itself in different areas of your life? Did it have an effect on your emotions, thoughts, or general well-being?

_____

_____

_____

_____

_____

What needs or desires were unfulfilled or neglected during this period of hunger?

_____

_____

_____

_____

_____

How did you respond to this hunger? Did you
find healthy ways to deal with it, or did you
engage in activities that perpetuated or
concealed it?

_____

_____

_____

_____

_____

_____

What lessons can you learn from this experience? How can you better recognize and respond to your hunger moving forward?

_____

_____

_____

_____

_____

_____

_____

NOTES

FEBRUARY
SNOW

In this chapter, the author gives insight into the transformational and healing power of snow and its connection to the concept of wintering.

The author starts the chapter by describing the excitement and anticipation that comes with the first snowfall of the year. She reminisces about her childhood experiences of snow and how it filled her with wonder and joy. Her relationship with snow, however, changed as she got older. She began to equate it with discomfort, coldness, and solitude, matching the negative emotions that may often accompany the winter season in our life.

The author points out how snow can change the environment by covering everything in a pristine layer of white. This transition represents the transformational power of rest and retreat during challenging times. May argues that, just as nature relies on the winter season to rest, regenerate, and prepare for new growth, humans need times of rest and solitude to heal and rejuvenate.

The author explores the therapeutic qualities of wintter, particularly the solitude it provides. She finds solace in taking solitary snow walks, describing how the hushed and muted landscape creates a sense of calm and reflection. Winter's stillness and silence allow for introspection and self-discovery, creating a place for inner development and healing.

The chapter also discusses the Danish idea of hygge, which encompasses comfort and happiness. May explains how the warmth and comfort of indoor spaces throughout the winter may aid in our healing and restoration. She emphasizes the importance of finding moments of pleasure and consolation even in the midst of challenging times.

In conclusion, May articulates brilliantly the fundamental relationship between snow, wintering, and the transforming power of rest and retreat. She advises individuals to embrace the wintering seasons in their own lives, to find peace in isolation, and to identify the possibilities for development and rejuvenation that can be discovered in these tough times using her own personal reflections.

Key Lessons

1. Embrace the beauty of winter: The chapter points out the importance of finding beauty and peace throughout the winter season. Despite the cold and harsh weather, there is a unique tranquility to be found in nature covered by snow. We can nurture a feeling of tranquility and gratitude even in tough circumstances by shifting our perspective and appreciating the beauty of winter.

2. Allow yourself to relax and retreat: Winter is a season that asks us to slow down, rest, and withdraw. It is important to recognize the importance of restorative periods in our life and to honor our need for solitude. We may tap into our inner resources and find strength to overcome challenging circumstances by surrendering to rest and retreat.

3. Seek the wisdom of nature: The chapter stresses the wisdom that can be gained from observing and connecting with nature. There are lessons to be gained about development, adaptability, and rebirth just as trees lose their leaves and animals hibernate during winter. We can find guidance and motivation for our own journeys by attuning ourselves in to the natural world.

4. The power of rituals: This chapter delves into the importance of winter rituals such as lighting a candle or gathering around a fire. During difficult times, rituals give a feeling of stability, comfort, and connection. By including rituals into our lives, we may give our everyday routines a sense of purpose and meaning, as well as offer peace and grounding.

5. Embrace vulnerability and surrender control: Winter may be a period of vulnerability as we face life's limitations and uncertainties. The chapter teaches us to embrace our vulnerability and surrender control over situations beyond our control. We can find acceptance and strength in surrendering to the ebb and flow of life by letting go of our need for control.

EXERCISE AND SELF REFLECTION QUESTIONS

Exercise 1: Snow Mindfulness Walk
Objective: To practice mindfulness and connect with nature during winter.

Instructions:
1. Find a local park, forest, or any other outdoor location with snow-covered ground.

2. Dress appropriately for the cold weather, including thick clothing, gloves, a cap, and waterproof shoes.

3. As you stroll, pay attention to the the details of the winter landscape around you - the texture of tree barks, the shapes of snowflakes, and the stillness in the air.

4. Fully engage your senses - feel the crispness of the cold air on your skin, listen to the sound of snow crunching beneath your feet, and take note of any scents or smells present.

5. Walk for at least 15-20 minutes, or longer if you feel comfortable.

6. After the walk, spend some time reflecting on your experience.
Write down your reflections on the following questions:

How did it feel to be totally present in nature?

_____

_____

_____

_____

_____

Did you notice anything new or surprising?

_____

_____

_____

_____

_____

How did the snow and winter atmosphere affect your mood or mindset?

_____

_____

_____

_____

Exercise 2: Snow Journaling

Objective: To reflect on personal experiences with snow and to examine the emotions and memories associated with it.

Instructions:

1. Find a peaceful and comfortable place where you can relax and concentrate on writing.
2. Create a winter-themed mood by playing quiet instrumental music or lighting a candle.
3. Write the word "snow" or draw a snowflake in the image below.

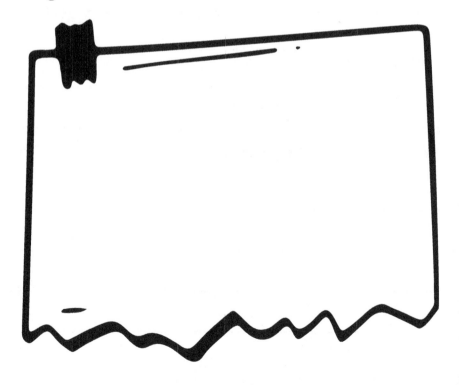

"Start writing freely about your particular snow experiences. It might be childhood memories, a recent snowfall, or other memorable experiences or feelings related with snow".

Allow yourself to delve into the sensory details.

How does snow feel, taste, smell, or sound to you?

_____

_____

_____

_____

Reflect on the emotions that snow creates in you.

Does it bring you joy, nostalgia, or a sense of calm?

_____

_____

_____

Do you have any unpleasant memories or relationships with snow?

_____

_____

_____

-Once you feel you have conveyed your thoughts and emotions regarding snow, take a minute to go over what you have written and ponder on it.

-Consider the role that snow plays in your life and how it affects your thinking throughout the winter months.

-If you feel comfortable, share any insights or thoughts that came throughout the exercise with a trusted friend or loved one.

NOTES

COLD WATER

The author reflects on the transformative impact of cold water and its connection to the concept of wintering in this chapter. She highlights the physical and psychological benefits of immersing oneself in cold water, as well as how it can help us face challenges with perseverance.

May starts by sharing her personal experience with the ice-cold sea. She recounts the initial shock and discomfort, which is followed by a sense of invigoration and heightened awareness. She compares it to the wintering process, in which accepting harsh or unpleasant events may contribute to one's personal growth and resilience. Cold water immersion becomes a metaphor for enduring and finding strength in challenging times.

Afterwards, the author explores the science of cold water immersion. She explains that the cold water stimulates our body's natural response mechanisms, causing endorphins to be released and our immune system to be strengthened. This not only helps our physical health but also our mental health by reducing stress, anxiety, and sadness. Cold water immersion may be seen as a type of self-care, a way of reconnecting with our body and embracing the present moment.

In addition, the author looks into the cultural and historical significance of cold water immersion. She highlights that various cultures have long recognized the therapeutic effects of cold water, from the ancient Greeks and Romans rejuvenating themselves with cold water baths to Nordic sauna traditions followed by plungings into icy lakes. This cultural context adds depth to the practice and emphasizes its universality and timelessness.

The author goes further into the metaphorical aspects of cold water immersion. Just as immersion in cold water may be painful but ultimately thrilling, going through tough times can lead to personal growth and resilience. May argues that embracing the pain and uncertainty of winter may be transformational in the long run, helping us to emerge stronger and more resilient.

Finally, May focuses on the physical, psychological, and metaphorical aspects of immersing oneself in cold water. She highlights the transformative power of embracing pain as well as the significance of self-care during challenging circumstances. May provides insights and inspiration for handling difficult times in our life by connecting the practice of cold water immersion to the concept of wintering. Finally, she encourages individuals to embrace the discomfort and growth that winter might bring, knowing that they will come out stronger and more resilient.

Key Lessons

1. The importance of embracing discomfort: The author highlights the transformative power of immersing oneself in uncomfortable situations. She learns to navigate discomfort with courage and resilience by facing the cold water through the winter. This lesson reminds us that when we push ourselves beyond our comfort zones, we often grow.

2. Rest as an act of defiance: The author discovers that taking time to rest and withdraw is an act of strength and rebellion against cultural demands, rather than a sign of weakness. In a culture that glorifies productivity and constant busyness, she learns the importance of prioritizing self-care and recognizing its healing power.

3. The power of human connection and community: As she joins a group of winter swimmers, the author realizes the importance of human connection and

community support. Bonds created as a result of shared experiences, such as swimming in cold water, may bring comfort and a feeling of belonging. This lesson emphasizes the importance of maintaining ties with people during difficult times.

4. Finding beauty in resilience: Despite the harshness of winter and the hardships it brings, the author experiences moments of extraordinary beauty. She learns to appreciate nature's resilience, finding solace in the frozen environment. This lesson teaches us to find beauty in the midst of challenges, reminding us that resilience and strength can be found in unexpected places.

5. The role of self-compassion in healing: The author explores the healing power of self-compassion throughout the chapter. She practices self-care and learns to listen to her body's demands by allowing herself to rest and retreat. This important lesson reminds us to be compassionate with ourselves during hard times, to recognize our own limitations, and to prioritize our own well-being.

SELF REFLECTION QUESTIONS

How has the concept of embracing "cold water" resonated with your personal experiences of rest and retreat during difficult times?

_____

_____

_____

_____

_____

How can you create a mindset of resilience and acceptance, recognizing that difficult times are an unavoidable part of life and can offer opportunities for growth and transformation?

_____

_____

_____

_____

_____

In what ways do you tend to judge or criticize yourself during stressful times? How can you exercise self-compassion and embrace self-care at these times?

_____

_____

_____

_____

_____

Are there any patterns or beliefs you have regarding rest and retreat that may be hindering your ability to completely embrace and benefit from these experiences? How can you challenge and reframe these beliefs?

_____

_____

_____

_____

_____

_____

_____

How can you apply the lessons from "Cold water" to your regular life, beyond just difficult times? How can you make rest and retreat a regular practice for general well-being and resilience?

_____

_____

_____

_____

_____

_____

NOTES

MARCH
SURVIVAL

In this chapter, the focus shifts to the theme of survival and resilience throughout difficult moments in our life. The author views March as a transitional month, when the darkness of winter begins to fade away, making room for new beginnings and growth.

May starts by reflecting on her own winter experiences and how it may be challenging for many people. She emphasizes the need to recognize and embrace the dormant periods in our life, as they may be critical times for reflection and growth. Wintering, according to May, teaches us resilience and the significance of embracing difficulties in order to emerge stronger.

As March approaches, the author describes the initial signs of spring, which provide hope and renewal. She focuses on on these tiny signs, such as the appearance of buds, birdsong, and the lengthening of the day, pointing out how they might be metaphorical for our own inner growth and healing. March becomes a symbol of survival and resilience as we learn to navigate through difficult times and begin to see tiny glimpses of change.

The author also delves into the concept of post-traumatic growth, describing how survival involves more than simply surviving or overcoming hardship, but also growing and learning from it. She says that by acknowledging and working through our challenges, we might find hidden strengths and insights that can shape our future.

During these times of survival, the author discusses the importance of community and support. She highlights the need of reaching out to people and enabling ourselves to lean on them when needed. May also highlights the need of empathy and understanding, both in giving and receiving, in navigating through difficult times.

Overall, the chapter examines the transforming power of embracing our challenges and finding strength in the process. The author offers a compelling perspective on how struggles can shape us for the better, teaching us resilience, empathy, and gratitude. By recognizing the signs of spring in our own lives, we can find hope, renewal, and a path forward.

Key Lessons

1. Embrace the idea of "wintering" as a metaphor for challenging moments in our lives: The chapter discusses the concept of "wintering" as a metaphor for difficult periods in our lives. By recognizing and embracing these times of difficulty, we may better navigate them and find opportunities for growth and renewal.

2. Recognize the importance of self-care: It is critical to prioritize self-care during the wintering season. Taking time to relax, refuel, and participate in things that bring us joy and comfort can help us survive tough times. Taking care of oneself is essential, whether it is by spending time in nature, indulging in a hobby, or seeking professional help.

3. Find solace in community and connection: Even in difficult situations, seeking help from others can be of great benefit. Finding solace in the support network around us may bring comfort, validation, and practical assistance, whether it's turning to family, friends, or joining a community of individuals facing similar challenges.

4. Nurture resilience and adaptability: The wintering

season can bring unexpected changes and challenges. Learning to adapt and bounce back from setbacks is essential for survival. Building resilience and embracing our adaptability helps us navigate challenging situations, fostering growth and ultimately leading us to a place of strength and renewal.

5. Embrace the transformational power of wintering: The chapter highlights that the wintering period is about more than simply survival; it is also about the possibility of change and growth. We can gain valuablel insights, learn important lessons, and emerge even stronger and more resilient if we embrace difficult seasons in our life. Wintering allows us to tap into our inner power and discover aspects of ourselves that we may not have known existed.

EXERCISE

Exploring the Power of Resilience

Objective: To develop resilience and find strength in challenging times.

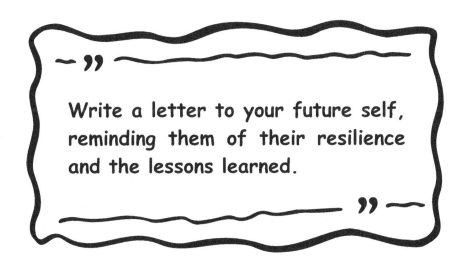

Write a letter to your future self, reminding them of their resilience and the lessons learned.

-Keep this letter somewhere visible, such as a pinboard or diary, as a reminder of your inner strength and ability to overcome challenges.

-Whenever you face new obstacles, look back to this letter and draw upon the lessons learnt to help you navigate through them.

SELF REFLECTION QUESTIONS

How do the author's experiences and insights in this chapter match with your own survival experiences in difficult times?

_____

_____

_____

_____

In light of the author's discussion of rest and retreat as survival tactics, what actions or changes can you make in your own life to prioritize rest and self-care during challenging periods?

_____

_____

_____

How does the author's exploration of survival challenge traditional notions of strength and resilience? How can you apply these alternative perspectives into your own understanding of survival?

What role do community and support play in the author's survival experiences during tough times? How can you build or develop your personal support network?

_____

_____

_____

_____

Reflect on the author's observations regarding the cyclical nature of survival, noting that bad days will eventually give way to better days. How can this perspective help you in maintaining optimism and resilience throughout your own "wintering" periods?

_____

_____

_____

_____

_____

NOTES

SONG

The author explores the transformational power of music during periods of difficulty. She starts by recounting her experience of walking in the snow and hearing a bird singing. This unexpected tune resonates deeply within her, bringing a moment of peace and reminding her of the world's inherent beauty.

The author looks into music's universal human connection and its ability to touch our souls. She discusses many musical experiences and memories, describing how music has the ability to transport us to different emotional states. Music creates a sense of belonging by connecting our inner world to the shared human experience.

The author delves into her own wintering experience, which she examines metaphorically throughout the book. She recalls instances in her life when she felt stuck, unconnected, and lost. She realizes that music has been her rock throughout these trying times. It has given her the power to survive and find peace in moments of darkness.

May reveals the science behind the emotional and psychological impact of music. It has the potential to increase the release of oxytocin, a hormone associated with bonding and relaxation. Music also triggers our brain's reward system, giving us pleasure as well as a sense of accomplishment. It may also synchronize our heart rates and breathing rhythms, enabling us to experience a collective energy and connection.

The author explores the role of music in community meetings and how it brings people together. Music has always been a strong force in promoting togetherness and shared experiences, from ancient rites to current concerts. It cuts beyond linguistic and cultural boundaries, communicating straight to our emotions.

May concludes the chapter by reflecting on the power of music to heal and lead us through tough times. A song may both elevate our spirits and assist us navigate darkest moments in ur lives. We may find strength, resilience, and hope by totally allowing ourselves to be fully present in the melody.

In conclusion, this chapter examines the transforming power of music. The author shares her own experience of finding consolation and connection through music throughout difficult times in her life. She reveals music's capacity to transcend barriers and communicate directly to our emotions by delving into its scientific and communal aspects. Music has the power to heal, elevate, and lead us through our darkest times, creating a feeling of oneness and reminding us of the world's intrinsic beauty. The chapter emphasizes the value of music as a source of solace and inspiration during tough times.

Key Lessons

1. Embrace the transforming power of music: The chapter highlights the transformative effect of music in tough circumstances. It teaches us to go to melodies and lyrics for peace, comfort, and inspiration. We may communicate our feelings, connect with others, and heal our spirits through singing. Music becomes a strong instrument for self-expression as well as a means of navigating through difficult events.

2. Seek solace in nature: The chapter shows how nature's songs may bring solace and guidance during trying times. She highlights the value of reconnecting with nature, which may provide peace, perspective, and a sense of belonging. We may find the strength to survive and embrace the cycles of life by immersing ourselves in nature's melodies.

3. Embrace the impermanence of seasons: The chapter explores how the changing seasons in nature mirror the stages of human existence. We may learn to accept the ups and downs of our own life by accepting the transience and impermanence of seasons. The lessons of "Song" inspire us to find beauty in the passing moments and to take solace in the knowledge that change is an essential aspect of development and rebirth.

4. Foster connections and community: The chapter points out the importance of communal sing-alongs in creating a feeling of belonging and togetherness. The author points out the transforming power of collective singing, highlighting the power of collective voices. It highlights the significance of fostering connections and building a supportive community in order to weather difficult times together.

5. Find your own tune: The chapter encourages individuals to find their own unique tune in life. Just as each bird has its own individual song, we should embrace our own authentic voice and freely express ourselves. It challenges the idea of conforming to cultural norms and encourages us to embrace our actual selves, cultivating self-acceptance and personal growth. We can navigate hard times with resilience and authenticity if we find our own tune.

EXERCISE

Exercise 1: Reflecting on Personal Song Lyrics

Objective: To explore the power of music and lyrics in expressing our emotions.

Instructions:

1. Take some time to think about a song that has resonated with you during a difficult time in your life.
2. Write down the lyrics of the song, or look them up if needed.
3. Reflect on the meaning behind the lyrics and how they relate to your own experiences.
4. Consider the emotions and feelings that this song evokes in you. How does it make you feel?
5. Write a short journal entry or create a piece of artwork expressing your thoughts and emotions related to this song.

SELF REFLECTION QUESTIONS

How does the concept of a "song" relate to your personal rest and retreat journey? What does it mean to discover and embrace your own distinct song?

_____

_____

_____

_____

_____

How have you seen the power of rest and retreat in enabling growth and renewal in your life? What examples can you think of when taking time to rest brought about positive change or insights?

_____

_____

_____

_____

_____

Have you ever felt the joy and liberation of fully expressing your own song in the midst of difficulties? How did it feel, and how can you cultivate more of these experiences in the future?

_____

_____

_____

_____

_____

_____

Are there any aspects of your life in which you feel out of sync or disconnected from your actual self? How might rest and retreat help you reconnect with and realign with your true aspirations and values?

_____

_____

_____

_____

_____

_____

What are some practical steps you might take to integrate more rest and retreat into your life, particularly during difficult times? How can you make time for reflection while yet completely embracing the power of winter?

_____

_____

_____

_____

_____

NOTES

EPILOGUE
LATE MARCH
THAW

The author concludes the book by reflecting on the themes explored throughout the chapters and offers insights and hope to individuals who are going through difficult times.

May starts by acknowledging the transformation brought about by winter. She shares her experience of the thaw in late March, when the ice melts, revealing the hidden depths of the world below. During difficult situations, this serves as a metaphor for personal growth and transformation. May highlights that tough times in our life, commonly referred to as "winters," may also provide opportunity for self-discovery and resilience.

The author revisits the idea of rest and retreat that have been explored n preceding chapters. She points out the importance of embracing these phases as an essential part of the human experience. May encourages individuals to resist the societal pressure to be constantly working and instead recognize the value of rest and stillness.

The author additionally highlights the importance of community and connection in overcoming challenges. She points out the importance of others' support and understanding during personal "winters." We may take comfort in knowing that we are not alone in our problems by sharing our stories and experiences.

In addition, the author dives into the concept of embracing uncertainty and the unknown. She says that rather than being afraid of these characteristics, we might learn to find comfort in them. By embracing life's uncertainties, we open ourselves up to new opportunities for growth.

In her final thoughts, the author extends a message of hope. She reminds readers that, although wintering is challenging, it is not permanent. Difficult times will pass, just as winter ultimately gives way to spring. May encourages readers to believe in the cyclical cycle of life, knowing that seasons of growth and renewal will always exist.

She concludes by reminding readers that wintering is a normal part of the human experience, not a failure or a sign of weakness. We have the chance to learn, heal, and grow during these times. May encourages us to accept our winters with compassion and seek the lessons and growth they offer.

May concludes her book with a profound and insightful message of hope and resilience, pointing out the importance of rest, community, and embracing uncertainty. She encourages individuals to embrace their own winters and find courage and growth in whatever challenges they experience. This epilogue is a perfect conclusion to a book that examines the significance of rest and retreat in navigating tough times and returning to the warmth and beauty of spring.

Key Lessons

1. Embrace life's cyclical nature: The chapter focuses on the concept of seasons and how life, like nature, operates in cycles. Just like winter is followed by spring, difficult times are ultimately followed by pleasant ones. Accepting this cyclical nature allows us to find peace and hope during difficult times.

2. Find strength in vulnerability: The author shares her own vulnerability, acknowledging that admitting when we are struggling and seeking assistance or support requires courage. Rather than seeing vulnerability as a sign of weakness, we might see it as a chance to connect with people, share our burdens, and grow in resilience.

3. Make time for rest and recovery: This chapter emphasizes the significance of taking breaks and resting, particularly during difficult times. Rest is not only refreshing, but it is also necessary for healing and regaining strength. We can navigate challenging times better and emerge stronger if we prioritize rest.

4. Appreciate the small joys in life: The author encourages finding joy in the small things in life, even when things are challenging. We may find peace, gratitude, and moments of relief by learning to appreciate the beauty of ordinary situations, which will help us persevere and find comfort in the midst of hardships.

5. Find strength in nature: Nature is a great source of inspiration, solitude, and renewal. The chapter encourages us to connect with nature, whether through walks in the woods, observing the seasons change, or just spending time outside. Nature reminds us of our natural resilience and flexibility, providing a reassuring perspective and a reminder that we are a part of something greater than ourselves. We may discover healing, calm, and renewed sense of strength by immersing ourselves in nature.

SELF REFLECTION QUESTIONS

How did the author's winter experiences, especially during the March thaw, demonstrate the gradual process of healing and growth? How can you apply this understanding to your own journey?

_____

_____

_____

_____

_____

In what ways did practicing rest and retreat contribue to the author's personal transformation and resilience? How can you adopt these practices into your own life in the moving forward?

_____

_____

_____

_____

_____

_____

_____

Reflecting on the idea of "Unraveling" as
discussed in the chapter, how have moments of
disintegration or breakdown led to growth and
self-discovery in your own life?

_____

_____

_____

_____

_____

How did the natural world and the changing seasons affect the author's wintering process? How can you develop a stronger connection to nature to help in your own healing and restoration?

_____

_____

_____

_____

_____

Think on the chapter's subject of community and interconnectedness. How have your connections with others been affected by the winter? How can you feed and build your support network during difficult times?

_____

_____

_____

_____

Reflect on the importance embracing uncertainty and the unknown, as discussed in the chapter. How can you develop a curious and open mindset in order to navigate difficult situations with greater resilience and adaptability?

NOTES

FINAL EVALUATION QUESTIONS

How has the concept of "wintering" helped you in understanding and navigating difficult times in your life?

_____

_____

_____

_____

What are some practical strategies you can apply to your everyday life to make room for rest and retreat?

_____

_____

_____

_____

How has this book challenged your assumptions about productivity and accomplishment?

_____

_____

_____

_____

Have you recognized any areas in your life where you resist taking the essential rest and retreat time? How do you intend to address such areas?

_____

_____

_____

_____

Do you agree with the author's perspective that wintering is both important and transformative? Why or why not?

_____

_____

_____

_____

How has reading this book influenced your attitude on self-care and the importance of mental and emotional well-being?

_____

_____

_____

_____

Can you identify any specific tips or advice given by the author that you intend to use in your own wintering experiences?

_____

_____

_____

_____

What role do community and support play in the wintering process? How can you build a support network for yourself in difficult times?

_____

_____

_____

Reflecting on your overall reading experience, how has Wintering impacted your approach to navigating and and embracing challenges in the future?

_____

_____

_____

NOTES

NOTES

NOTES

Made in the USA
Las Vegas, NV
04 January 2025

15893872R00095